YOUR KNOWLEDGE HAS VALUE

- We will publish your bachelor's and master's thesis, essays and papers

- Your own eBook and book - sold worldwide in all relevant shops

- Earn money with each sale

Upload your text at www.GRIN.com
and publish for free

Florian Rübener

Review of the movie "Lantana"

GRIN Publishing

Bibliographic information published by the German National Library:

The German National Library lists this publication in the National Bibliography; detailed bibliographic data are available on the Internet at http://dnb.dnb.de .

Imprint:

Copyright © 2006 GRIN Verlag, Open Publishing GmbH
Print and binding: Books on Demand GmbH, Norderstedt Germany
ISBN: 978-3-640-79651-9

This book at GRIN:

http://www.grin.com/en/e-book/163922/review-of-the-movie-lantana

GRIN - Your knowledge has value

Since its foundation in 1998, GRIN has specialized in publishing academic texts by students, college teachers and other academics as e-book and printed book. The website www.grin.com is an ideal platform for presenting term papers, final papers, scientific essays, dissertations and specialist books.

Visit us on the internet:

http://www.grin.com/

http://www.facebook.com/grincom

http://www.twitter.com/grin_com

Universität Duisburg-Essen
Cultural Studies: Filming Australia
SS 06
18.08.2006

Review of

Lantana

Florian Rübener

Table of contents

1. Introduction

1.1 Overview

Directed by

Ray Lawrence

Cast

Anthony LaPaglia	...	*Detective Leon Zat*
Kerry Armstrong	...	*Sonja Zat*
Rachel Blake	...	*Jane O'May*
Glenn Robbins	...	*Pete O'May*
Barbara Hershey	...	*Dr. Valerie Sommers*
Geoffrey Rush	...	*John Knox*
Vince Colosimo	...	*Nik Daniels*
Daniella Farinacci	...	*Paula Daniels*
Peter Phelps	...	*Patrick Phelan*
Leah Purcell	...	*Detective Claudia Wiss*

Release date

2001

Lantana is an Australian film that was released in 2001 and directed by Ray Lawrence. It is based on Andrew Bovell's play *Speaking In Tongues*. The movie is set in a suburban area of Sydney and portrays the lives of nine different characters focusing especially on their relationships and their individual struggle with emotions. The name *Lantana* means the plant Lantana, a very thick and tangled shrub. The title can be interpreted as a metaphor for the tangled, intertwined relationships that are presented in the film.

Lantana was the first movie that won all of the top six categories of the Australian Film Institute (AFI) awards: best picture, best director, best actress, best actor, best supporting actress, best supporting actor.[1]

1.2 Plot summary

Lantana tells the story of eight couples who are joined through sex, betrayal and death. The four marriages are between Leon and Sonja, Jane and Pete, Nik and Paula, and Valerie and John.

The central event in *Lantana* is the mysterious death of psychiatrist Dr. Valerie Sommers, her body is found in a remote forrest near a quiet back road. Detective Leon Zat is called to solve the case and during his investigations he discovers that his wife Sonja was one of Valerie's clients because of their unfulfilling marriage. Leon suspects Valerie's husband John Knox, who claims he wasn't at home when his wife desperatley called him from a phone box, saying her car broke down, to be involved in his wife's death. Leon finds out that John and Valerie had their own difficulties with their relationship based on the murder of their daughter Eleanor and Valerie's suspicion of John having an affair with her latest client, Patrick.

Leon's investigations lead to an awkward situation with Jane O'May, a woman he has a short-term affair with. She finds a crucial clue, one of Valerie's shoes, in the shrubs of her neighbour Nik, a seemingly loving father and husband.

It turns out that Valerie had an accident and Nik picked her up intending to drive her home. But when Nik spontaneously took a shortcut Valerie paniced an jumped out of the car. Nik didn't mean to scare her so he just left her there in the forrest but later he found her shoe in his car.

---

[1] See http://www.imdb.com (the Internet Movie Data Base)

2. The characters of Lantana

2.1 The characters and their little secrets

Detective Leon Zat

Detective Leon Zoat is a tough, middle-aged police officer who suffers from some sort of midlife-crisis. He is presented as a stereo-typed, Australian male; strong and unable to express his feelings.

He deceives his wife Sonja by beginning a short-term affair with Jane, a woman he met at the dancing course he's attending with his wife. His marriage suffers from routine and Leon has built himself a fassade of pretence and faked happiness. Though he still loves Sonja he is not able to express his feelings for her.

His suppressed emotions tend to be released at his job as a cop in form of uncontrollable aggression towards criminals. The scene were we see him beat up a suspect for being a drug dealer is the first where Leon's emotional state becomes somehow visible and we see that he is suffering and does not know how to cope with his feelings. His emotional state becomes more apparent when he confronts Patrick and his lover in their appartment, he overreacts and is again very aggressive. His colleague Claudia then points out, "your marriage is falling apart and so are you." Leon has to face challenges not only in his marriage but also with his physical condition, he has a weak heart.

Sonja Zat

Sonja appears to be a lively person but in fact she's overwhelmed by desperation. Although she has a husband and two kids she feels lost and lonely, thinking her marriage lacks passion, challenges and most of all emotional honesty. Like Leon she hides her emotions but attends therapist Valerie Sommers, unknowing to her husband. During her therapy sessions she reveals to suspect Leon of having an affair but points out that she wouldn't see the affair itself as betrayel but the fact that Leon might not tell her about it. In order to reanimate passion Sonja and Leon attend to a Latin dancing class and this is ironically where their marriage goes off the tracks as it is here that Leon meets Jane.

Jane O'May

Jane has recently split up from her husband and lives on her own again, searching for love. She really likes Leon and hopes for more than just an affair but has to discover that Leon does not share her feelings. She's still got strong feelings for her ex-husband and is also attracted to her neighbour Nik. Jane is honest and sincere but cares too much for other people's business which leads to a conflict with her friend Paula, Nik's wife.

Dr. Valerie Sommers

Valerie can be considered the central figure in *Lantana* because her death is the link that intertwines all plots and relationships. She is a successful psychologist but because of the tragic loss of her daughter she has become needy and fragile.

Since their daughter Eleanor was murdered Valerie and her husband John have begun to alienate and Valerie shares the same desperation as Sonja. Valerie finds her marriage lacking sensuality and passion. She has just begun to see a new client, a man named Patrick and there is an awkward tension between them. Valerie hates that Patrick has an affair with a married man but more than that she fears that it could be her own husband. As the therapy sessions with Patrick go on Valerie starts more and more to question her relationship to John and falls into deep depression. One night she has an accident and tries to call John for help several times but he just won't answer the phone. Valerie figures he's not at home and leaves messages on his answering machine then she disappears.

John Knox

Valerie's husband John is a very quiet and reserved person. He doesn't show a lot of interest in Valerie's work or her sorrows. When she tries to explain what's so awkward about her and Patrick, John simply responds „Well, refer him off". John disapproves of the book Valerie wrote about their daughter's death and Valerie thinks that he doesn't miss her at all. It turns out that John frequently visits the place where Eleanor's body was found bringing along some flowers, all that unknowing to Valerie. Like Leon, John has been unfaithful in his marriage and deceived Valerie.

Nik Daniels

Nik and his wife Paula life next door to Jane and Nik is also an old friend of Jane's former husband Pete. Nik is a very caring and loving father and husband but gets under suspicion of having killed Valerie as Jane sees him throwing one of her shoes into the shrubs. He is the stereotypical unemployed male who tends to drink a bit and he is always seen either walking the baby or fixing the car and is mainly characterised by these actions.

Paula Daniels

Nik's wife Paula works hard to raise her children properly. She does a lot of extra work as her and Nik depend only on her income. She is quite jealous and probably feels threatened by her friend Jane who invited Nik to come over whe she wasn't at home. Paula loves Nik unconditionally and is desperate to see him after he got arrested. Even though it seems like Nik really killed Valerie Paula takes sides for him and trusts him.

We see the relationship between Paula and Jane is already tenuous as Paula does not trust her around Nik. However their friendship is finally destroyed when Jane tidies up Paula's house while her and Nik are at the police station and Paula screams across the fence, " you've got no right, no fucking right."

Patrick Phelan

Patrick is a gay man and Valerie Sommer's latest client. He tells her about a married man he's having an affair with and how he feels treated secondarily after the man's wife. While Valerie tries her best to convince him that he's doing something wrong he sees himself as a victim insisting on the man leaving his wife. Patrick challenges Valerie because she personally dislikes what he's doing furthermore she suspects her own husband to be Patrick's affair. The sessions with Patirck make Valerie reconsider her own marriage and when Patrick tells her that his male lover uses him as a refuge from his wife and that his lover doesn't like having sex with her, she starts to worry about her husband. Patrick sees love as a game and he does not accept to be on the losers' side.

<u>Detective Claudia Wiss</u>

Claudia is a colleague and friend of Leon. The audience doesn't get to know her that well but we see that she has a secret crush on some stranger she sees frequently at her favourite restaurant.

2.2 The troubled marriages in Lantana

<u>Leon and Sonja</u>

The relationship of Leon and Sonja suffers from routine. While Sonja tries to bring back fun and passion into their marriage Leon seems to lack enthusiasm. At their dance course Sonja is having a good time while Leon acts stiff and seems uninteressted.

What Sonja misses most in her life is emotional honesty but Leon can't or maybe doesn't want to share his feelings with her, he's looking for „love" without any commitment and obligations and starts an affair with Jane.

<u>Valerie and John</u>

Since the death of their daughter the relationship of Valerie and John has become very cold and unsensual. John doesn't show any interest in Valerie or her work but she is very needy for attention and love and feels negelcted and ignored as a result of his repulse.

Valerie complains that they barely sleep together and feels that sleeping with her is unpleasant for John. When Patrick tells her that his male lover doesn't like having sex with his wife, she suspects John to be Patrick's lover because he won't look at her when they have sex.

In the end Valerie dies because of John's ignorance. When she calls for help after her accident he pretends to be not a home and leaves her desperate calls unanswered.

<u>Nik and Paula</u>

The only intact marriage presented in *Lantana* seems to be the one of Nik and Paula. They are both honest, caring and supportive to each other. Nik tells Paula for instance that Jane invited him for coffee altough he didn't have to and Paula, stricken with jealousy; tells Jane to stay away from her husband. When Nik gets arrested

Paula almost freaks out in the police station trying to see Nik and does not hesitate to believe in his innocence. Although they are both still very young and financially troubled they're capable of raising three kids without losing their passion for each other. After all what they've been through they manage to trust each other and to stay togehter, they are the only couple with trust between them which all the other couples lack. When Leon witnesses this unconditional acceptance it makes him feel uncomfortable as it is lacking in his marriage and he leaves the room.

<u>Jane and Pete</u>

Jane and Pete live seperated but aren't divorced yet. Though Jane has an affair with Leon and a crush on Nik she still seems to have feelings for Pete and so does he for her. It is quite obvious that Jane still feels something for Pete as she does not take off her wedding ring after their split.

It is not clear if Jane and Pete really end up togehter again as the final scene of *Lantana* shows Jane dancing alone in her apartment.

3. Lantana: The movie

3.1 The main aspects of Lantana

Lantana is all about trust and betrayel. There are Nik and Paula who trust each other unconditionally and there is Leon who deceives his wife. There is an obvious contrast between the marriage of Nik and Paula and that of Leon and Sonja. While Paula believes in Nik's innocence just on his own words Sonja doubts that Leon is faithful and distrusts him. The contrast is shown again when John asks Leon what holds his marriage together, "loyalty...love...maybe habit, sometimes passion... our kids." There is no mention of trust as Leon has already lied to John about being faithful after which John confesses that he was unfaithful too in his own marriage.

There is another form of betrayel presented by Valerie and John. Their relationship is only held together by grief but there is no emotional honesty, they have reached a dead point at their marriage but aren't able to admit it.

Another aspect of *Lantana* are the unsolved issues all characters have to face. They all have guilt to work through. Leon has to work through the guilt of his affair, Nik of not saying anything to the police about picking Valerie up and scaring her accidentally and John because he was at home when Valerie called and didn't do anything to help her. Jane has to face her destroyed friendship with Paula and her broken marriage with Pete. Valerie's death brings out the worst of all relationships including her own.

3.2 How does Lantana work as a movie?

Lantana is a very branched an twisted movie that could be described as a patchwork film as different plots are mixed and combined to a whole throughout the movie.

We first meet Leon at the beginning of his affair with Jane and run throughout the movie experiencing the situation mainly through his emotions. As the movie goes on we learn more about the other characters and it seems like Leon has some connection to all of them. He has an affair with Jane who is separated from Pete who Leon meets accidently in a bar, he is married to Sonja who is seeing Valerie who is a psychologist married to John who is the first suspect in her disappearance. Leon passes Nik when he leaves Jane's house at the end of their affair and Nik is married to Paula and they are Jane's next door neighbours. Leon comes into contact with all the characters at some point in the movie and so it seems like he is the main protagonist.

As the story continues we learn more about the other characters and their lives and relationships. Before we learn too much about Leon the viewpoint changes and we meet his wife Sonja talking to Valerie about her marriage. But we don't spend that much time with Sonja as the viewpoint changes rapidly and we learn about Valerie and the loss of her daughter, Eleanor, who was murdered eighteen months ago. The story changes quickly from one character to another, giving the audience only a slight insight in their individual lives. We do not get close to any of the characters until we have met them and experienced some of their pain and how twisted the relationships are.

What makes *Lantana* stand out from classic Hollywood love movies is the number of plots that are mixed together. There's not only one but four to five different storylines in *Lantana* and none of them can be classified as the main story. There are neither major nor minor characters as everybody contributes important details to the movie as a whole. Although Leon appears to be the main protagonist within the movie because of his apparent connection to all of the characters, the real connection turns out to be Valerie as her disappearance shows the deceit within the marriages. But not only the characters deceit each other, the audience is deceived as well. Through the movie we develop certain expectations, we belive that Nik could possibly be Valerie's murderer or that John is Patrick's lover. In the end the audience has to realise that everything is much less obvious that expected and that the movie plays tricks with them leaving wrong clues. Certain things are kept in the dark and *Lantana* does not explain everything right form the beginning. The movie is built around the mystery of Valerie's death and gives the impression of being a modern detective story as it is up to Leon and the audience to decipher the clues. But it is actually a film about love, sex, trust and betrayel and reflects the way the relationships are intertwined through these factors. *Lantana* can be seen as a pschological study of the australien middle-class, focusing on five relationships.

The Lantana plant represents how entwined the relationships are without the characters realising it.

3.3 Winners and losers in the game of love

At some point of the movie Patrick says that love is a game and in the conclusion we can see some of the characters on the winners' and the losers' side. Some find love, some reanimate their love, others continue deceiving their partner and some are literally left out in the rain. Nik and Paula continue happily, Pete and Jane continue their separation and John is forced to cope with both his daughter's and his wife's deaths. Patrick has to realise that there is no future for him and his lover, he watches him happy with his family and his exclusion is emphasised by him standing in the rain.

Claudia finally meets her secret love in the restaurant and Leon is forced to confront his guilt and emotions, he confesses his affair to Sonja and both have to fix their broken marriage.

3.4 Comment

Lantana is a highly entertaining movie that benefits most from the deep and ambiguous characters. All characters have a cross to bare, they all have certain issues and problems to cope with what enables the audience to identify with them to some extend. None of the characters appears as a good-natured and pure-hearted hero, they are all ordinary people facing a conflict and they all possess a dark side.

The plot is twisting and turning through the movie and nothing turns out the way it seemed at the beginning, and the mystery of Valerie's death adds a lot of suspense to the movie. *Lantana* definitely stands out because of it's unusual genre mix of a love story, a crime story and a psychological drama. It is dramatic, thrilling and humorous at the same time.

Although *Lantana* is apparently a love movie there is no trace of kitsch in it, the relationships are all imperfect, realistic and human. *Lantana* does not provide the audience with a rather typical Hollywood-like happy ending where all characters get the love they're longing for. Like in real life certain obstacles remain and not all problems and crises are dissolved.